Plant Name | **Date Planted**

Water Requirements 💧 💧💧 💧💧💧

Sunlight ☀ ☽ ●

☐ Seed   ☐ Transplant

Date	Event

Notes

Outcome

Uses

Purchased at: _____   Price: _____

Plant Name	Date Planted

Water Requirements 💧　💧💧　💧💧💧

Sunlight ☀ ◐ ●

☐ Seed　　☐ Transplant

Date	Event

Notes

Outcome

Uses

Purchased at: _____ Price: _____

Plant Name | **Date Planted**

Water Requirements 💧 💧💧 💧💧💧

Sunlight ☀ ☼ ●

☐ Seed   ☐ Transplant

Date	Event

Notes

Outcome

Uses

Purchased at: _____   Price: _____

Plant Name	Date Planted

Water Requirements 💧 💧💧 💧💧💧

Sunlight ☀ ☼ ●

☐ Seed   ☐ Transplant

Date	Event

Notes

Outcome

Uses

Purchased at: _____   Price: _____

Plant Name   **Date Planted**

Water Requirements 💧 💧💧 💧💧💧   Sunlight ☀ ☼ ●

☐ Seed   ☐ Transplant

Date	Event

Notes

Outcome

Uses

Purchased at: _____   Price: _____

Plant Name	Date Planted

Water Requirements 💧 💧💧 💧💧💧   Sunlight ☀ ◐ ●

☐ Seed   ☐ Transplant

Date	Event

Notes

Outcome

Uses

Purchased at: _____   Price: _____

Plant Name   **Date Planted**

Water Requirements 💧 💧💧 💧💧💧   Sunlight ☀ ☽ ●

☐ Seed   ☐ Transplant

Date	Event

Notes

Outcome

Uses

Purchased at: _____   Price: _____

Plant Name	Date Planted

Water Requirements 💧 💧💧 💧💧💧

Sunlight ☀ ◐ ●

☐ Seed ☐ Transplant

Date	Event

Notes

Outcome

Uses

Purchased at: _____ Price: _____

Plant Name	Date Planted

Water Requirements 💧 💧💧 💧💧💧

Sunlight ☀ ☼ ●

☐ Seed   ☐ Transplant

Date	Event

Notes

Outcome

Uses

Purchased at: _____   Price: _____

Plant Name	Date Planted

Water Requirements 💧 💧💧 💧💧💧   Sunlight ☀ ☽ ●

☐ Seed   ☐ Transplant

Date	Event

Notes

Outcome

Uses

Purchased at: _____   Price: _____

Plant Name	Date Planted

Water Requirements 💧 💧💧 💧💧💧   Sunlight ☀︎ ☼ ●

☐ Seed   ☐ Transplant

Date	Event

Notes

Outcome

Uses

Purchased at: _____   Price: _____

Plant Name		Date Planted	

Water Requirements 💧 💧💧 💧💧💧

Sunlight ☀ ☼ ●

☐ Seed   ☐ Transplant

Date	Event

Notes

Outcome

Uses

Purchased at: _____   Price: _____

Plant Name	Date Planted

Water Requirements 💧 💧💧 💧💧💧

Sunlight ☀ ☼ ●

☐ Seed ☐ Transplant

Date	Event

Notes

Outcome

Uses

Purchased at: _____ Price: _____

Plant Name	Date Planted

Water Requirements 💧 💧💧 💧💧💧

Sunlight ☀ ◐ ●

☐ Seed   ☐ Transplant

Date	Event

Notes

Outcome

Uses

Purchased at: _____   Price: _____

Plant Name	Date Planted

Water Requirements 💧 💧💧 💧💧💧   Sunlight ☀ ◐ ●

☐ Seed   ☐ Transplant

Date	Event

Notes

Outcome

Uses

Purchased at: _____   Price: _____

Plant Name	Date Planted

Water Requirements 💧 💧💧 💧💧💧

Sunlight ☀ ☽ ●

☐ Seed ☐ Transplant

Date	Event

Notes

Outcome

Uses

Purchased at: _____ Price: _____

Plant Name	Date Planted

Water Requirements 💧 💧💧 💧💧💧   Sunlight ☀ ☼ ●

☐ Seed   ☐ Transplant

Date	Event

Notes

Outcome

Uses

Purchased at: _____   Price: _____

Plant Name	Date Planted

Water Requirements 💧 💧💧 💧💧💧

Sunlight ☀ ☀ ●

☐ Seed ☐ Transplant

Date	Event

Notes

Outcome

Uses

Purchased at: _____ Price: _____

Plant Name	Date Planted

Water Requirements 💧 💧💧 💧💧💧   Sunlight ☀ ☼ ●

☐ Seed   ☐ Transplant

Date	Event

Notes

Outcome

Uses

Purchased at: _____   Price: _____

Plant Name	Date Planted

Water Requirements 💧 💧💧 💧💧💧   Sunlight ☀ ◐ ●

☐ Seed   ☐ Transplant

Date	Event

Notes

Outcome

Uses

Purchased at: _____   Price: _____

Plant Name	Date Planted

Water Requirements 💧 💧💧 💧💧💧   Sunlight ☀ ☽ ●

☐ Seed   ☐ Transplant

Date	Event

Notes

Outcome

Uses

Purchased at: _____   Price: _____

Plant Name	Date Planted

Water Requirements 💧 💧💧 💧💧💧   Sunlight ☀ ☼ ●

☐ Seed   ☐ Transplant

Date	Event

Notes

Outcome

Uses

Purchased at: _____   Price: _____

Plant Name **Date Planted**

Water Requirements 💧 💧💧 💧💧💧   Sunlight ☀ ☾ ●

☐ Seed   ☐ Transplant

Date	Event

Notes

Outcome

Uses

Purchased at: _____   Price: _____

Plant Name	Date Planted

Water Requirements 💧 💧💧 💧💧💧　　Sunlight ☀ 🌤 ●

☐ Seed　　☐ Transplant

Date	Event

Notes

Outcome

Uses

Purchased at: _____　　Price: _____

Plant Name	Date Planted

Water Requirements 💧 💧💧 💧💧💧

Sunlight ☀ ☼ ●

☐ Seed   ☐ Transplant

Date	Event

Notes

Outcome

Uses

Purchased at: _____   Price: _____

Plant Name	Date Planted

Water Requirements 💧 💧💧 💧💧💧   Sunlight ☀ ☼ ●

☐ Seed   ☐ Transplant

Date	Event

Notes

Outcome

Uses

Purchased at: _____   Price: _____

Plant Name	Date Planted

Water Requirements 💧 💧💧 💧💧💧

Sunlight ☀ ☼ ●

☐ Seed   ☐ Transplant

Date	Event

Notes

Outcome

Uses

Purchased at: _____   Price: _____

Plant Name	Date Planted

Water Requirements 💧 💧💧 💧💧💧   Sunlight ☀ ◐ ●

☐ Seed   ☐ Transplant

Date	Event

Notes

Outcome

Uses

Purchased at: _____   Price: _____

Plant Name	Date Planted

Water Requirements 💧 💧💧 💧💧💧   Sunlight ☀ ☼ ●

☐ Seed   ☐ Transplant

Date	Event

Notes

Outcome

Uses

Purchased at: _____   Price: _____

Plant Name	Date Planted

Water Requirements 💧 💧💧 💧💧💧

Sunlight ☀ ☼ ●

☐ Seed   ☐ Transplant

Date	Event

Notes

Outcome

Uses

Purchased at: _____   Price: _____

Plant Name		Date Planted	

Water Requirements 💧 💧💧 💧💧💧

Sunlight ☀ ☼ ●

☐ Seed   ☐ Transplant

Date	Event

Notes

Outcome

Uses

Purchased at: _____   Price: _____

Plant Name	Date Planted

Water Requirements 💧 💧💧 💧💧💧

Sunlight ☀ ◐ ●

☐ Seed   ☐ Transplant

Date	Event

Notes

Outcome

Uses

Purchased at: _____   Price: _____

Plant Name   **Date Planted**

Water Requirements 💧 💧💧 💧💧💧   Sunlight ☀ ☽ ●

☐ Seed   ☐ Transplant

Date	Event

Notes

Outcome

Uses

Purchased at: _____   Price: _____

Plant Name	Date Planted

Water Requirements 💧 💧💧 💧💧💧

Sunlight ☀ ☼ ●

☐ Seed   ☐ Transplant

Date	Event

Notes

Outcome

Uses

Purchased at: _____   Price: _____

Plant Name	Date Planted

Water Requirements 💧 💧💧 💧💧💧

Sunlight ☀ ☽ ●

☐ Seed ☐ Transplant

Date	Event

Notes

Outcome

Uses

Purchased at: _____ Price: _____

Plant Name	Date Planted

Water Requirements 💧 💧💧 💧💧💧

Sunlight ☀ ☼ ●

☐ Seed ☐ Transplant

Date	Event

Notes

Outcome

Uses

Purchased at: _____ Price: _____

Plant Name	Date Planted

Water Requirements 💧 💧💧 💧💧💧

Sunlight ☀ ◐ ●

☐ Seed ☐ Transplant

Date	Event

Notes

Outcome

Uses

Purchased at: _____ Price: _____

Plant Name	Date Planted

Water Requirements 💧 💧💧 💧💧💧   Sunlight ☀ ☼ ●

☐ Seed   ☐ Transplant

Date	Event

Notes

Outcome

Uses

Purchased at: _____   Price: _____

Plant Name	Date Planted

Water Requirements 💧 💧💧 💧💧💧   Sunlight ☀️ 🌤️ ⚫

☐ Seed   ☐ Transplant

Date	Event

Notes

Outcome

Uses

Purchased at: _____   Price: _____

Plant Name	Date Planted

Water Requirements 💧 💧💧 💧💧💧

Sunlight ☀ ☼ ●

☐ Seed   ☐ Transplant

Date	Event

Notes

Outcome

Uses

Purchased at: _____   Price: _____

Plant Name

Date Planted

Water Requirements 💧 💧💧 💧💧💧

Sunlight ☀ ☼ ●

☐ Seed   ☐ Transplant

Date	Event

Notes

Outcome

Uses

Purchased at: _____   Price: _____

Plant Name	Date Planted

Water Requirements 💧 💧💧 💧💧💧   Sunlight ☀ ◐ ●

☐ Seed   ☐ Transplant

Date	Event

Notes

Outcome

Uses

Purchased at: _____   Price: _____

Plant Name	Date Planted

Water Requirements 💧 💧💧 💧💧💧

Sunlight ☀ ☼ ●

☐ Seed ☐ Transplant

Date	Event

Notes

Outcome

Uses

Purchased at: _____ Price: _____

Plant Name	Date Planted

Water Requirements 💧 💧💧 💧💧💧

Sunlight ☀ ◐ ●

☐ Seed   ☐ Transplant

Date	Event

Notes

Outcome

Uses

Purchased at: _____   Price: _____

Plant Name	Date Planted

Water Requirements 💧 💧💧 💧💧💧   Sunlight ☀ ☼ ●

☐ Seed   ☐ Transplant

Date	Event

Notes

Outcome

Uses

Purchased at: _____   Price: _____

Plant Name	Date Planted

Water Requirements 💧 💧💧 💧💧💧

Sunlight ☀ ☼ ●

☐ Seed ☐ Transplant

Date	Event

Notes

Outcome

Uses

Purchased at: _____ Price: _____

Plant Name **Date Planted**

Water Requirements 💧 💧💧 💧💧💧   Sunlight ☀ ☼ ●

☐ Seed ☐ Transplant

Date	Event

Notes

Outcome

Uses

Purchased at: _____ Price: _____

Plant Name	Date Planted

Water Requirements 💧 💧💧 💧💧💧   Sunlight ☀ ☼ ●

☐ Seed   ☐ Transplant

Date	Event

Notes

Outcome

Uses

Purchased at: _____   Price: _____

Plant Name	Date Planted

Water Requirements 💧 💧💧 💧💧💧   Sunlight ☀ 🌤 ●

☐ Seed   ☐ Transplant

Date	Event

Notes

Outcome

Uses

Purchased at: _____   Price: _____

Plant Name	Date Planted

Water Requirements 💧 💧💧 💧💧💧

Sunlight ☀ ◐ ●

☐ Seed   ☐ Transplant

Date	Event

Notes

Outcome

Uses

Purchased at: _____   Price: _____

Plant Name   **Date Planted**

Water
Requirements 💧 💧💧 💧💧💧   Sunlight ☀ ☀ ●

☐ Seed   ☐ Transplant

Date	Event

Notes

Outcome

Uses

Purchased at: _____   Price: _____

Plant Name	Date Planted

Water Requirements 💧 💧💧 💧💧💧

Sunlight ☀ ☼ ●

☐ Seed   ☐ Transplant

Date	Event

Notes

Outcome

Uses

Purchased at: _____   Price: _____

Plant Name	Date Planted

Water Requirements 💧 💧💧 💧💧💧   Sunlight ☀ ◐ ●

☐ Seed   ☐ Transplant

Date	Event

Notes

Outcome

Uses

Purchased at: _____   Price: _____

Plant Name	Date Planted

Water Requirements 💧 💧💧 💧💧💧   Sunlight ☀ ☾ ●

☐ Seed   ☐ Transplant

Date	Event

Notes

Outcome

Uses

Purchased at: _____   Price: _____

Plant Name		Date Planted	

Water Requirements 💧 💧💧 💧💧💧

Sunlight ☀ ☀/🌒 ●

☐ Seed   ☐ Transplant

Date	Event

Notes

Outcome

Uses

Purchased at: _____   Price: _____

Plant Name	Date Planted

Water Requirements 💧 💧💧 💧💧💧

Sunlight ☀ ◐ ●

☐ Seed   ☐ Transplant

Date	Event

Notes

Outcome

Uses

Purchased at: _____   Price: _____

Plant Name	Date Planted

Water Requirements 💧 💧💧 💧💧💧   Sunlight ☀ ☼ ●

☐ Seed   ☐ Transplant

Date	Event

Notes

Outcome

Uses

Purchased at: _____   Price: _____

Plant Name	Date Planted

Water Requirements 💧 💧💧 💧💧💧   Sunlight ☀ ◐ ●

☐ Seed   ☐ Transplant

Date	Event

Notes

Outcome

Uses

Purchased at: _____   Price: _____

Plant Name   **Date Planted**

Water Requirements 💧 💧💧 💧💧💧   Sunlight ☀ ☼ ●

☐ Seed   ☐ Transplant

Date	Event

Notes

Outcome

Uses

Purchased at: _____   Price: _____

Plant Name	Date Planted

Water Requirements 💧 💧💧 💧💧💧   Sunlight ☀ ☽ ●

☐ Seed   ☐ Transplant

Date	Event

Notes

Outcome

Uses

Purchased at: _____   Price: _____

Plant Name **Date Planted**

Water Requirements 💧 💧💧 💧💧💧

Sunlight ☀ ☼ ●

☐ Seed ☐ Transplant

Date	Event

Notes

Outcome

Uses

Purchased at: _____ Price: _____

Plant Name	Date Planted

Water Requirements 💧 💧💧 💧💧💧

Sunlight ☀ 🌤 ●

☐ Seed ☐ Transplant

Date	Event

Notes

Outcome

Uses

Purchased at: _____ Price: _____

Plant Name **Date Planted**

Water Requirements 💧 💧💧 💧💧💧   Sunlight ☀ ☽ ●

☐ Seed ☐ Transplant

Date	Event

Notes

Outcome

Uses

Purchased at: _____ Price: _____

Plant Name	Date Planted

Water Requirements 💧 💧💧 💧💧💧   Sunlight ☀ ☼ ●

☐ Seed   ☐ Transplant

Date	Event

Notes

Outcome

Uses

Purchased at: _____   Price: _____

Plant Name   **Date Planted**

Water
Requirements 💧 💧💧 💧💧💧   Sunlight ☀ ☽ ●

☐ Seed   ☐ Transplant

Date	Event

Notes

Outcome

Uses

Purchased at: _____   Price: _____

Plant Name	Date Planted

Water Requirements 💧 💧💧 💧💧💧   Sunlight ☀ ☼ ●

☐ Seed   ☐ Transplant

Date	Event

Notes

Outcome

Uses

Purchased at: _____   Price: _____

Plant Name	Date Planted

Water Requirements 💧 💧💧 💧💧💧   Sunlight ☀ 🌤 ●

☐ Seed   ☐ Transplant

Date	Event

Notes

Outcome

Uses

Purchased at: _____   Price: _____

Plant Name	Date Planted

Water Requirements 💧 💧💧 💧💧💧   Sunlight ☀ ◐ ●

☐ Seed   ☐ Transplant

Date	Event

Notes

Outcome

Uses

Purchased at: _____   Price: _____

Plant Name | **Date Planted**

Water Requirements 💧 💧💧 💧💧💧

Sunlight ☀ ☼ ●

☐ Seed   ☐ Transplant

Date	Event

Notes

Outcome

Uses

Purchased at: _____   Price: _____

Plant Name	Date Planted

Water Requirements 💧 💧💧 💧💧💧   Sunlight ☀ ☼ ●

☐ Seed   ☐ Transplant

Date	Event

Notes

Outcome

Uses

Purchased at: _____   Price: _____

Plant Name	Date Planted

Water Requirements 💧 💧💧 💧💧💧

Sunlight ☀ ☼ ●

☐ Seed   ☐ Transplant

Date	Event

Notes

Outcome

Uses

Purchased at: _____   Price: _____

Plant Name   **Date Planted**

Water Requirements 💧   💧💧   💧💧💧   Sunlight ☀ ☼ ●

☐ Seed   ☐ Transplant

Date	Event

Notes

Outcome

Uses

Purchased at: _____   Price: _____

Plant Name   **Date Planted**

Water Requirements 💧 💧💧 💧💧💧   Sunlight ☀ ☼ ●

☐ Seed   ☐ Transplant

Date	Event

Notes

Outcome

Uses

Purchased at: _____   Price: _____

Plant Name	Date Planted

Water Requirements 💧 💧💧 💧💧💧

Sunlight ☀︎ ◐ ●

☐ Seed ☐ Transplant

Date	Event

Notes

Outcome

Uses

Purchased at: _____ Price: _____

Plant Name | **Date Planted**

Water Requirements 💧 💧💧 💧💧💧

Sunlight ☀ ☼ ●

☐ Seed   ☐ Transplant

Date	Event

Notes

Outcome

Uses

Purchased at: _____   Price: _____

Plant Name	Date Planted

Water Requirements 💧 💧💧 💧💧💧

Sunlight ☀ ◐ ●

☐ Seed   ☐ Transplant

Date	Event

Notes

Outcome

Uses

Purchased at: _____   Price: _____

Plant Name **Date Planted**

Water Requirements 💧 💧💧 💧💧💧

Sunlight ☀️ ☼ ●

☐ Seed   ☐ Transplant

Date	Event

Notes

Outcome

Uses

Purchased at: _____   Price: _____

Plant Name	Date Planted

Water Requirements 💧 💧💧 💧💧💧

Sunlight ☀ ☾ ●

☐ Seed   ☐ Transplant

Date	Event

Notes

Outcome

Uses

Purchased at: _____   Price: _____

Plant Name		Date Planted

Water Requirements 💧 💧💧 💧💧💧

Sunlight ☀ ☼ ●

☐ Seed   ☐ Transplant

Date	Event

Notes

Outcome

Uses

Purchased at: _____   Price: _____

Plant Name	Date Planted

Water Requirements 💧 💧💧 💧💧💧   Sunlight ☀ ◐ ●

☐ Seed   ☐ Transplant

Date	Event

Notes

Outcome

Uses

Purchased at: _____   Price: _____

Plant Name		Date Planted	

Water Requirements 💧 💧💧 💧💧💧

Sunlight ☀ ☼ ●

☐ Seed ☐ Transplant

Date	Event

Notes

Outcome

Uses

Purchased at: _____ Price: _____

Plant Name	Date Planted

Water Requirements 💧 💧💧 💧💧💧

Sunlight ☀️ 🌤️ ⚫

☐ Seed ☐ Transplant

Date	Event

Notes

Outcome

Uses

Purchased at: _____ Price: _____

Plant Name | **Date Planted**

Water Requirements 💧 💧💧 💧💧💧

Sunlight ☀ ☼ ●

☐ Seed ☐ Transplant

Date	Event

Notes

Outcome

Uses

Purchased at: _____ Price: _____

Plant Name	Date Planted

Water Requirements 💧 💧💧 💧💧💧

Sunlight ☀️ 🌤️ ⚫

☐ Seed   ☐ Transplant

Date	Event

Notes

Outcome

Uses

Purchased at: _____ Price: _____

Plant Name	Date Planted

Water Requirements 💧 💧💧 💧💧💧   Sunlight ☀ ☼ ●

☐ Seed   ☐ Transplant

Date	Event

Notes

Outcome

Uses

Purchased at: _____   Price: _____

Plant Name	Date Planted

Water Requirements 💧 💧💧 💧💧💧

Sunlight ☀ ☼ ●

☐ Seed ☐ Transplant

Date	Event

Notes

Outcome

Uses

Purchased at: _____ Price: _____

Plant Name	Date Planted

Water Requirements 💧 💧💧 💧💧💧   Sunlight ☀ ☼ ●

☐ Seed   ☐ Transplant

Date	Event

Notes

Outcome

Uses

Purchased at: _____   Price: _____

Plant Name	Date Planted

Water Requirements 💧　💧💧　💧💧💧

Sunlight ☀ ☼ ●

☐ Seed　　☐ Transplant

Date	Event

Notes

Outcome

Uses

Purchased at: _____　Price: _____

Plant Name   **Date Planted**

Water Requirements 💧 💧💧 💧💧💧   Sunlight ☀ ☽ ●

☐ Seed   ☐ Transplant

Date	Event

Notes

Outcome

Uses

Purchased at: _____   Price: _____

Plant Name	Date Planted

Water Requirements 💧 💧💧 💧💧💧   Sunlight ☀ ☼ ●

☐ Seed   ☐ Transplant

Date	Event

Notes

Outcome

Uses

Purchased at: _____   Price: _____

Plant Name | **Date Planted**

Water Requirements 💧 💧💧 💧💧💧

Sunlight ☀ ☀ ●

☐ Seed   ☐ Transplant

Date	Event

Notes

Outcome

Uses

Purchased at: _____   Price: _____

Plant Name	Date Planted

Water Requirements 💧 💧💧 💧💧💧

Sunlight ☀ ◐ ●

☐ Seed   ☐ Transplant

Date	Event

Notes

Outcome

Uses

Purchased at: _____ Price: _____

Plant Name　　　　　　　　　　**Date Planted**

Water Requirements 💧　💧💧　💧💧💧　　　Sunlight ☀️ 🌤 ⚫

☐ Seed　　☐ Transplant

Date	Event

Notes

Outcome

Uses

Purchased at: _____　Price: _____

Plant Name	Date Planted

Water Requirements 💧 💧💧 💧💧💧   Sunlight ☀ ☼ ●

☐ Seed   ☐ Transplant

Date	Event

Notes

Outcome

Uses

Purchased at: _____   Price: _____

Plant Name | **Date Planted**

Water Requirements 💧 💧💧 💧💧💧   Sunlight ☀ ☼ ●

☐ Seed   ☐ Transplant

Date	Event

Notes

Outcome

Uses

Purchased at: _____   Price: _____

Plant Name	Date Planted

Water Requirements 💧 💧💧 💧💧💧   Sunlight ☀ ☼ ●

☐ Seed   ☐ Transplant

Date	Event

Notes

Outcome

Uses

Purchased at: _____   Price: _____

Plant Name   **Date Planted**

Water Requirements 💧 💧💧 💧💧💧   Sunlight ☀ ☼ ●

☐ Seed   ☐ Transplant

Date	Event

Notes

Outcome

Uses

Purchased at: _____   Price: _____

Plant Name	Date Planted

Water Requirements 💧 💧💧 💧💧💧   Sunlight ☀ ◐ ●

☐ Seed   ☐ Transplant

Date	Event

Notes

Outcome

Uses

Purchased at: _____   Price: _____

Plant Name	Date Planted

Water Requirements 💧 💧💧 💧💧💧   Sunlight ☀ ☼ ●

☐ Seed   ☐ Transplant

Date	Event

Notes

Outcome

Uses

Purchased at: _____   Price: _____

Plant Name	Date Planted

Water Requirements 💧 💧💧 💧💧💧

Sunlight ☀ ☼ ●

☐ Seed   ☐ Transplant

Date	Event

Notes

Outcome

Uses

Purchased at: _____   Price: _____

Plant Name   **Date Planted**

Water
Requirements 💧 💧💧 💧💧💧   Sunlight ☀ ◐ ●

☐ Seed   ☐ Transplant

Date	Event

Notes

Outcome

Uses

Purchased at: _____   Price: _____

Plant Name	Date Planted

Water Requirements 💧 💧💧 💧💧💧   Sunlight ☀ ☼ ●

☐ Seed   ☐ Transplant

Date	Event

Notes

Outcome

Uses

Purchased at: _____   Price: _____

Plant Name | **Date Planted**

Water Requirements 💧 💧💧 💧💧💧

Sunlight ☀ ☼ ●

☐ Seed ☐ Transplant

Date	Event

Notes

Outcome

Uses

Purchased at: _____ Price: _____

Plant Name　　　　　　　　　　　　**Date Planted**

Water Requirements 💧　💧💧　💧💧💧

Sunlight ☀ ◐ ●

☐ Seed　　☐ Transplant

Date	Event

Notes

Outcome

Uses

Purchased at: _____　　Price: _____

Plant Name | **Date Planted**

Water Requirements 💧 💧💧 💧💧💧

Sunlight ☀ ☼ ●

☐ Seed   ☐ Transplant

Date	Event

Notes

Outcome

Uses

Purchased at: _____   Price: _____

Plant Name	Date Planted

Water Requirements 💧 💧💧 💧💧💧   Sunlight ☀ ☼ ●

☐ Seed   ☐ Transplant

Date	Event

Notes

Outcome

Uses

Purchased at: _____   Price: _____

Plant Name | **Date Planted**

Water Requirements 💧 💧💧 💧💧💧

Sunlight ☀ ☼ ●

☐ Seed   ☐ Transplant

Date	Event

Notes

Outcome

Uses

Purchased at: _____   Price: _____

Plant Name	Date Planted

Water Requirements 💧 💧💧 💧💧💧   Sunlight ☀ ☼ ●

☐ Seed   ☐ Transplant

Date	Event

Notes

Outcome

Uses

Purchased at: _____   Price: _____

Plant Name		Date Planted	

Water Requirements 💧 💧💧 💧💧💧

Sunlight ☀ ☀ ●

☐ Seed   ☐ Transplant

Date	Event

Notes

Outcome

Uses

Purchased at: _____   Price: _____

Plant Name	Date Planted

Water Requirements 💧 💧💧 💧💧💧

Sunlight ☀ ☼ ●

☐ Seed   ☐ Transplant

Date	Event

Notes

Outcome

Uses

Purchased at: _____   Price: _____

Plant Name	Date Planted

Water Requirements 💧 💧💧 💧💧💧   Sunlight ☀ ☼ ●

☐ Seed   ☐ Transplant

Date	Event

Notes

Outcome

Uses

Purchased at: _____   Price: _____

Plant Name	Date Planted

Water Requirements 💧 💧💧 💧💧💧

Sunlight ☀ ☼ ●

☐ Seed ☐ Transplant

Date	Event

Notes

Outcome

Uses

Purchased at: _____ Price: _____

Plant Name	Date Planted

Water Requirements 💧 💧💧 💧💧💧   Sunlight ☀ ☽ ●

☐ Seed   ☐ Transplant

Date	Event

Notes

Outcome

Uses

Purchased at: _____   Price: _____

Plant Name	Date Planted

Water Requirements 💧 💧💧 💧💧💧   Sunlight ☀ ◐ ●

☐ Seed   ☐ Transplant

Date	Event

Notes

Outcome

Uses

Purchased at: _____   Price: _____

Plant Name

Date Planted

Water Requirements 💧 💧💧 💧💧💧

Sunlight ☀ ☼ ●

☐ Seed   ☐ Transplant

Date	Event

Notes

Outcome

Uses

Purchased at: _____   Price: _____

Plant Name	Date Planted

Water Requirements 💧 💧💧 💧💧💧

Sunlight ☀ ☼ ●

☐ Seed   ☐ Transplant

Date	Event

Notes

Outcome

Uses

Purchased at: _____   Price: _____

Plant Name	Date Planted

Water Requirements 💧 💧💧 💧💧💧   Sunlight ☀ ☼ ●

☐ Seed   ☐ Transplant

Date	Event

Notes

Outcome

Uses

Purchased at: _____   Price: _____

Plant Name	Date Planted

Water Requirements 💧 💧💧 💧💧💧

Sunlight ☀ ☼ ●

☐ Seed　　☐ Transplant

Date	Event

Notes

Outcome

Uses

Purchased at: _____　Price: _____

Plant Name	Date Planted

Water Requirements 💧 💧💧 💧💧💧   Sunlight ☀ ☽ ●

☐ Seed   ☐ Transplant

Date	Event

Notes

Outcome

Uses

Purchased at: _____   Price: _____

Plant Name	Date Planted

Water Requirements 💧 💧💧 💧💧💧   Sunlight ☀ ☼ ●

☐ Seed   ☐ Transplant

Date	Event

Notes

Outcome

Uses

Purchased at: _____   Price: _____

www.ingramcontent.com/pod-product-compliance
Lightning Source LLC
LaVergne TN
LVHW012115070526
838202LV00056B/5740